REST TO RISE

The Art of Strategic Hibernation

Dr Mukesh Aggarwal

Made with on the Notion Press Platform
www.notionpress.com

CONTENTS

PREFACE

In today's fast-paced world, success is often equated with relentless action, constant hustle, and the sacrifice of rest. We are led to believe that the more we do, the more we achieve. But what if true growth lies not in endless activity but in the strategic balance between effort and renewal? What if our greatest potential is unlocked when we learn to harness the power of pause?

Rest to Rise: The Art of Strategic Hibernation challenges the conventional wisdom of success by offering a new paradigm—one where rest is not a retreat but a key to rising stronger, achieving more, and living with purpose. In this book, I delve into the transformative concept of "strategic hibernation"—a deliberate, purposeful approach to rest that fuels both personal and professional growth.

Drawing from science, psychology, and timeless wisdom, this book explores the critical role that physical, mental, and spiritual rest plays in our journey toward excellence. It reveals how rest is not the enemy of productivity but its secret weapon, one that sharpens creativity, resilience, and innovation.

From the restorative power of physical rest to the mental breakthroughs that come from mindful stillness, Rest to Rise guides you through the art of building momentum through recovery. You will discover how to time your pauses for maximum impact, how to align your purpose with restful living, and how to sustain a cycle of renewal that not only prevents burnout but propels you toward greater achievement.

This is a book for the ambitious and driven, for those who seek success without sacrificing well-being. It is for anyone who has felt the weight of constant motion and wondered if there might be a better way—a way to rise higher by embracing the art of doing nothing.

As you turn these pages, I invite you to reconsider the role of rest in your life and career. Rest is not a luxury or a sign of weakness; it is a powerful tool for growth and success. The time has come to pause, reflect, and rise to your fullest potential.

Welcome to the art of strategic hibernation.

—Dr. Mukesh Aggarwal

CHAPTER 1

INTRODUCTION

HIBERNATION IS A NECESSARIES PAUSE

In the natural world, hibernation is an extraordinary survival strategy. As winter settles in and food becomes scarce, animals retreat into a deep state of rest. During this time, their bodies slow down, conserving energy and resources. For many creatures, hibernation is not just a passive state of inactivity; it is a necessary pause that enables them to survive the harshest conditions and emerge in the spring, renewed and ready to thrive.

In our modern, fast-paced world, the idea of taking a deliberate pause might seem counterintuitive. With constant demands on our time and energy, we often equate success with continuous effort, pushing ourselves to the limit in the belief that more action equals more achievement. Yet, just as nature reminds us, there is immense power in the pause.

Rest, for humans, is not simply about relaxation. It is a strategic break—a time to recalibrate, recharge, and prepare for growth. The very act of stepping back can be transformative, allowing us to gain clarity, recover our strength, and set the stage for our next leap forward. This is the essence of strategic hibernation.

The Natural Cycle: From Hibernation To Bloom

Consider the cycles of nature: winter hibernation prepares animals for the abundance of spring. During the cold months, a bear's body enters a state of deep rest, its metabolic rate dropping, heart slowing, and energy conserved. But this period of dormancy is far from wasted time. Beneath the surface, essential processes are happening—healing, strengthening, and restoring. When the warmth of spring arrives, the bear emerges, fully prepared to make the most of the new season's opportunities.

We, too, follow cycles, whether we realize it or not. Our bodies, minds, and spirits require periods of rest to function optimally. Just as the bear's hibernation is a survival tactic, our own pauses—whether they take the form of short breaks, vacations, or even extended sabbaticals—are vital to our long-term success. Without them, we risk burning out, depleting our resources, and missing out on the opportunity to grow.

Rest as a Tool for Growth

What distinguishes strategic hibernation from ordinary rest is the intent behind it. Rather than viewing rest as a passive activity—a mere escape from the grind—it becomes a purposeful part of our personal and professional lives. It is the recognition that stepping back is not a retreat from progress but an essential phase of it. Just as athletes understand the importance of recovery for building strength, we must embrace the idea that renewal leads to transformation.

Research shows that periods of rest improve cognitive function, boost creativity, and enhance decision-making abilities. When we allow ourselves time to disengage from our routine tasks, we gain perspective. We begin to see solutions to problems that once seemed insurmountable. We find energy for new projects, and we rediscover the motivation to pursue our goals with renewed passion.

A Strategic Pause for Transformation

Imagine your life as a series of seasons. There are times of intense productivity, where you're focused and pushing toward your goals. But there must also be seasons of pause—moments where you allow yourself to rest, reflect, and recharge. These pauses are not wasted time; they are periods of preparation for your next phase of growth. Like the bear emerging from hibernation, you come back stronger, more focused, and ready to seize new opportunities.

In this book, we will explore the art of strategic hibernation. We'll delve into the science behind rest and renewal, drawing parallels between human behavior and nature's rhythms. You'll learn how to harness the power of pauses to fuel both your personal and professional success. By the end, you'll understand that rest isn't the opposite of productivity; it is an essential part of it.

In the chapters that follow, we'll explore practical strategies for integrating rest into your life—whether you're looking to boost creativity, enhance decision-making, or simply prevent burnout. Through stories, examples, and insights, you'll discover how to turn the power of pause into your secret weapon for rising to new heights.

The time to rest is not later—it's now. Welcome to the art of strategic hibernation. Welcome to Rest to Rise.

CHAPTER 2

THE SCIENCE OF REST
HOW DOWNTIME FUELS SUCCESS

In today's fast-paced world, rest is often undervalued. The hustle culture pushes us to keep going, but science tells us that downtime is not just a luxury—it's essential for success. Neuroscience shows that the brain needs rest to reorganize, recharge, and ultimately, to excel.

The Neuroscience behind Rest

The brain is an intricate organ, operating on billions of neural connections. These connections, or neural pathways, allow us to process information, solve problems, and create new ideas. But, just like any complex machine, the brain requires regular maintenance. That's where rest comes in.

Rest, whether in the form of sleep, meditation, or even daydreaming, activates something called the default mode network (DMN). The DMN is a group of brain regions that light up when we're not focused on external tasks, allowing our minds to wander. This "mental downtime" is crucial for making sense of the information we've absorbed throughout the day.

Sleep: The Ultimate Reset Button

Sleep is perhaps the most powerful form of rest. During deep sleep, the brain doesn't just shut down. Instead, it works on consolidating memories, strengthening neural pathways, and clearing out toxins that accumulate throughout the day. Research shows that sleep deprivation hinders cognitive function, impairs judgment, and diminishes creativity.

One fascinating finding in neuroscience is the role of REM (Rapid Eye Movement) sleep in creativity. REM sleep allows for unconventional connections between ideas, sparking creative breakthroughs. That's why a good night's sleep can lead to a fresh perspective on a problem that seemed unsolvable the day before.

Meditation: A Pathway to Clarity

Meditation, another form of rest, also has profound effects on the brain. Studies using MRI scans show that regular meditation strengthens the prefrontal cortex—the area responsible for decision-making and problem-solving. Moreover, meditation reduces activity in the amygdala, the brain's fear center, fostering emotional stability and resilience.

In the long run, meditative practices can increase gray matter in the brain, leading to enhanced cognitive function. By giving your mind time to focus inward, you allow it to reset, leading to better clarity and focus.

Daydreaming: The Power of Mind-Wandering

Even daydreaming, something often dismissed as unproductive, plays an essential role in brain function. When we let our minds wander, we engage the DMN, which helps process emotions, reflect on past experiences, and imagine future possibilities. This mental state is crucial for creativity because it allows disparate ideas to come together in unexpected ways.

Psychologists have found that individuals who spend time daydreaming are often more creative and better at problem-solving. Daydreaming creates mental space for innovation by letting the subconscious mind connect seemingly unrelated concepts.

Case Study: How Successful Figures Used Rest to Innovate

Let's take a closer look at how some of the world's most successful figures have harnessed the power of rest to fuel their success.

z

Albert Einstein: One of the greatest scientific minds, Einstein was known for taking long walks and indulging in naps during his workday. These breaks weren't just about relaxation. Einstein believed that these moments of rest allowed his subconscious mind to work on problems in the background. In fact, it was during such periods of rest that Einstein famously conceptualized some of his most groundbreaking ideas, including the theory of relativity.

Bill Gates: The co-founder of Microsoft has long been an advocate for taking time off to think deeply. Gates famously takes "think weeks," where he disconnects from daily distractions and spends time alone reading, reflecting, and contemplating the future. These rest periods have been credited with helping Gates think creatively about technology and philanthropy. By strategically stepping away from the grind, Gates has been able to foster new ideas that have revolutionized industries.

Dr. APJ Abdul Kalam: The Missile Man's Power of Reflection

Dr. APJ Abdul Kalam, India's beloved former President and renowned scientist, was known for his relentless work ethic. Yet, he also believed in the power of reflection and solitude. Dr. Kalam would often take time away from his busy schedule to read, meditate, and walk along the seashores of Rameswaram, his hometown. These moments of rest and introspection allowed him to clear his mind, make sense of complex problems, and foster creativity. Dr. Kalam credited these moments of quiet contemplation with helping him innovate and strategize during crucial moments in his career, including his work on India's missile development programs.

Narayana Murthy: Finding Balance Through Mindfulness
Narayana Murthy, the co-founder of Infosys, one of India's largest IT services companies, is another example of someone who embraced rest as a path to success. Despite the pressures of building a global empire, Murthy practiced mindfulness and meditation regularly. He has openly spoken about how meditation helped him maintain focus, emotional stability, and resilience in the face of business challenges. By taking time to recharge through mindfulness, Murthy was able to steer Infosys through both technological transformations and economic uncertainties, cementing his legacy as a visionary leader.

How Downtime Fuels Success

The examples of Einstein and Gates are not isolated cases. Many successful individuals have recognized the importance of downtime for productivity and innovation. Whether it's through sleep, meditation, or taking a walk, giving the brain time to rest allows for the mental restructuring needed for breakthroughs.
When we rest, the brain enters a state of consolidation, where it strengthens the connections between ideas and prunes unnecessary information.

This process is essential for long-term learning, memory retention, and problem-solving. Without rest, the brain becomes overloaded, leading to burnout and diminishing creative potential.

Strategic Hibernation for Success

Rest is not about being lazy; it's about strategic hibernation. Just as animals hibernate to conserve energy and survive harsh conditions, we can use rest as a tool to sharpen our minds, refuel our creativity, and navigate the challenges of life more effectively. The science is clear: rest fuels success.

By understanding and embracing the neuroscience of rest, we can learn to harness its power in our own lives. When we give ourselves permission to rest, we unlock the brain's full potential, allowing for innovation, clarity, and emotional well-being.

In the following chapter, we will delve into how to build rest into your routine without feeling guilty. We'll explore practical strategies for incorporating downtime into even the busiest schedules, ensuring you rise stronger after every pause.

CHAPTER 3

STRATEGIC HIBERNATION

TIMING YOUR REST FOR MAXIMUM IMPACT

Strategic hibernation is not about simply stopping when you're tired; it's about pausing at the right moments to recharge and gain perspective, so you can return stronger and more focused.

The Power of Strategic Rest

Many of us believe that success is a direct result of constant effort. The more hours we log, the closer we get to our goals. But the truth is, working without breaks can lead to diminishing returns. Fatigue sets in, creativity dwindles, and the very thing we're trying to achieve—progress—slips through our fingers.

Strategic hibernation, much like how animals prepare for winter, is about conserving energy when needed and using rest as a tool to fuel future performance. The key is timing—knowing when to push forward and when to pull back.

The Importance of Pivotal Breaks

Taking a break when you're at your lowest energy point may help you recover, but it's not the most effective approach to long-term productivity. True strategic hibernation happens when you pause at pivotal moments—those times when a brief rest can exponentially increase your clarity and energy for the next phase of your journey.

Imagine you're climbing a mountain. You can push yourself relentlessly toward the summit, but at some point, exhaustion will set in, and the risk of burnout becomes high. However, if you rest at key checkpoints—strategically chosen moments—your body and mind will have the chance to recuperate, making the journey to the top smoother and more sustainable.

The Art of Knowing When to Push Forward and When to Pull Back

The key to effective strategic hibernation lies in mastering the art of timing. Here are a few ways to gauge when it's time to push forward and when to pull back:

Mental Fatigue vs. Physical Fatigue: Are you physically exhausted, or is it more about your mental state? Physical fatigue can often be overcome with a short break or a good night's sleep. But mental fatigue often calls for deeper rest—time away from the very things that are draining your energy.

Creative Blocks: If you've hit a creative block, it's often a sign that you need to step away. Your brain needs time to digest information and reorganize it in a way that produces new ideas. Instead of pushing harder when creativity stalls, take a break and return with a fresh perspective.

Overwhelm vs. Underwhelm: Overwhelm is a clear signal that it's time to pull back and recharge. But equally important is recognizing when you're underwhelmed or uninspired. In these moments, rather than forcing yourself to stay productive, take a break to gain new insights and inspiration. Sometimes stepping away for a while allows you to return with renewed enthusiasm.

Practical Tools for Strategic Hibernation

Now that we understand the importance of taking breaks at pivotal moments, let's explore some practical tools to help you plan productive rest.

1. The Pomodoro Technique: Small, Frequent Breaks

The Pomodoro Technique is a time-management method that encourages short bursts of focused work, followed by a brief break. Here's how it works:

Set a timer for 25 minutes (one "Pomodoro").
Work on a task with full focus for the entire duration.
When the timer goes off, take a 5-minute break.

After four Pomodoros, take a longer break (15–30 minutes).

This technique allows for frequent mental breaks, ensuring that you maintain high levels of productivity without burning out. The key is consistency—those small pauses between work sessions can have a significant cumulative effect on your energy and focus.

2. Seasonal Breaks: Aligning Rest with Natural Cycles

In many cultures, seasons are seen as natural cycles of work and rest. Winter is often associated with slowing down and reflecting, while spring and summer bring renewed energy and growth. You can apply this concept to your life by planning seasonal breaks.

Take time off during the year to rest in alignment with natural rhythms. For instance, you might choose to hibernate in the winter months—whether by taking a vacation or simply slowing down your workload—and then ramp up your activities in the spring and summer. This approach allows you to work with the ebb and flow of your energy rather than against it.

3. Sabbaticals: Deep Rest for Long-Term Growth

Sometimes, we need more than just a weekend off or a few scattered breaks. A sabbatical is an extended period of rest or time away from work, usually lasting several weeks to several months. While traditionally associated with academia, sabbaticals are becoming more common in various fields.

The goal of a sabbatical is not only to rest but also to pursue personal development, explore new interests, or gain a fresh perspective on life. It's a chance to step out of the day-to-day grind and engage in deep rest and reflection. Whether it's a month off to travel or a few months to study something new, sabbaticals are a powerful way to recharge and return to work with a renewed sense of purpose.

Strategic Hibernation for Long-Term Success

Strategic hibernation is about more than just knowing when to rest; it's about understanding how rest fits into the broader picture of success. When you can strategically time your breaks, you maximize their impact on your productivity and creativity. It's not about working harder—it's about working smarter, using rest as a tool to propel you forward.

The next time you find yourself at a pivotal moment, ask yourself: Is it time to push forward, or is it time to pull back? Embrace the power of strategic hibernation, and you'll find that rest is not a detour from success—it's an essential part of the journey.

CHAPTER 4

THE REST-RISE CYCLE

BUILDING MOMENTUM THROUGH RECOVERY

Concept:
Life and success operate in cycles—ebbs and flows. Just like nature, where there are seasons of growth and seasons of rest, our personal and professional lives must follow a similar rhythm for sustained progress. Without proper rest, we run the risk of burnout, exhaustion, and stagnation. On the other hand, intentional recovery creates the space for creative breakthroughs, clarity, and new opportunities. This chapter explores how recovery is not just a passive retreat but an active investment in our future potential.

Imagine a farmer diligently working through planting season, carefully sowing seeds and nurturing the soil. After weeks of hard labor, the crop begins to sprout, but it is during the rest period between planting and harvesting that nature works its magic. The soil replenishes itself, rain nourishes the fields, and unseen growth takes place underground. This is the Rest-Rise Cycle. Much like farming, our work requires periods of focused effort, followed by rest and rejuvenation. The balance between rest and action is crucial for long-term growth and success.

Key Insight 1: Rest is Not a Pause, It's Part of the Plan

Rest is often misunderstood as an idle or unproductive state. We tend to think of it as time lost, when in reality, rest is an integral part of any growth strategy. Without it, we deplete our mental, emotional, and physical resources, making it harder to sustain high performance. The cycle of rest and rise isn't about taking a break from progress; it's about setting the stage for future success.

When we rest, we create the conditions for new ideas and solutions to emerge. Our minds are free to wander and explore possibilities that might not come to us when we are hyper-focused on daily tasks. Like the moon in its phases, our minds operate in cycles—there's a time for illumination and a time for quiet reflection. Each part of the cycle is necessary to maintain momentum in our personal and professional endeavors.

Metaphor: The Lunar Cycle

The phases of the moon offer a natural metaphor for understanding the importance of rest. The new moon represents a time of darkness, a period where we may feel less productive or in need of recuperation. As the moon waxes, light gradually returns, signaling the rise of energy, creativity, and action. Eventually, the full moon represents peak performance, a time when our hard work and ideas are fully realized. But after the full moon comes the waning phase—a necessary reduction in intensity that prepares us for the next cycle of renewal. Much like the lunar cycle, rest gives us the quiet space we need to recharge, while the rise phase reflects our energy in action.

Key Insight 2: Rest Fuels Breakthroughs

Many of the world's greatest discoveries and innovations have come during moments of rest or relaxation. Albert Einstein famously solved complex problems during walks or while playing the violin. Archimedes shouted "Eureka!" not while at work, but while relaxing in his bath. Why? Because creativity flourishes when we allow our minds to shift into a more relaxed, unfocused state. Our subconscious continues working on problems, making connections and formulating insights that we simply cannot access when we're constantly "on."

Our brains need downtime. Studies have shown that people who take breaks and rest are more likely to experience creative breakthroughs than those who work non-stop. Taking time to recharge doesn't mean we're abandoning our goals; rather, it provides the energy and clarity needed to achieve them. Just as the ocean ebbs and flows, so too must our mental and physical energy. The rhythm of rest fuels the rhythm of progress.

Key Insight 3: Rest as a Strategic Tool for Long-Term Success

In the world of sports, athletes follow training regimens that emphasize recovery as much as they do intense training. Why? Because overworking the body leads to injury, while well-planned recovery allows muscles to repair and grow stronger. The same principle applies to our personal growth and professional success. Continuous effort without recovery leads to diminishing returns.

In the context of our careers and creative pursuits, rest allows us to zoom out, reassess our direction, and ensure we're aligned with our larger goals. It offers the mental space to see the bigger picture, evaluate progress, and make necessary adjustments. Without rest, we may find ourselves stuck in the weeds, focusing on trivial tasks rather than strategic moves that drive momentum.

Metaphor: The Harvesting Cycle

Think of your work life as a garden. There are seasons of planting—where you lay the foundation for growth, putting in hard work, setting goals, and pushing forward. Then comes the resting season, where the garden needs time to rest, to be nourished by rain and sunlight, and to let growth happen beneath the surface. The harvest doesn't come immediately after planting; it arrives only after this necessary period of rest and recovery. Just like a farmer who knows to trust the process, we must learn to trust our own cycles of rest and rise.

Key Insight 4: Balance is the Key to Sustainable Momentum

The Rest-Rise Cycle is not about choosing between rest or productivity; it's about embracing both as complementary forces. Just as day cannot exist without night, success cannot thrive without recovery. Finding this balance ensures that we can sustain momentum over the long term, rather than burning out after short bursts of intense effort.

Much like a wave rising and falling in the ocean, our energy naturally oscillates between highs and lows. By respecting these rhythms, we can maximize our productivity during peak times and recover fully during slower periods. True success is not about how much we can do at once but how consistently we can rise after taking the time to rest.

Conclusion: Harness the Power of the Cycle

The Rest-Rise Cycle teaches us that recovery is not a weakness or a detour—it's the essential counterpart to growth and momentum. To rise to new heights in our lives, we must first learn to rest strategically. Like the seasons, nature's rhythms, or the lunar cycle, our own success requires a balance of action and recovery.

CHAPTER 5

REST FOR THE BODY

PHYSICAL RENEWAL FOR PEAK PERFORMANCE

In our relentless pursuit of success, we often overlook one of the most crucial elements of high performance—physical rest. While society glorifies hard work and long hours, there is a growing understanding among top athletes, entrepreneurs, and thought leaders that sustained peak performance is impossible without proper recovery. Physical rest not only heals the body but also replenishes our energy levels and enhances overall productivity.

The Science of Rest and Recovery

The human body is an extraordinary machine, designed to endure and adapt to stress. However, like any machine, it requires time to repair and refuel. Physical rest is essential to repairing tissues, building muscle, and optimizing brain function. A lack of it leads to fatigue, cognitive decline, and eventually burnout. Proper rest allows for physical recovery, better mental clarity, and improved decision-making.

Modern science shows that rest can elevate our energy levels by allowing the body's systems to reset. When we sleep, the body repairs cells, clears out toxins, and strengthens neural connections, all of which contribute to better health and peak performance.

The Role of Sleep in Physical Restoration

Sleep is the cornerstone of physical renewal. Research indicates that deep sleep stages, particularly REM (Rapid Eye Movement) sleep, are critical for repairing muscles, restoring brain function, and regulating hormones. Without sufficient sleep, our immune system weakens, stress levels rise, and our cognitive abilities decline. Top performers, like LeBron James and Tom Brady, understand the importance of sleep for their physical and mental performance. Both athletes credit much of their longevity and success to their strict sleep schedules and recovery routines.

Incorporating rest into your daily routine doesn't mean you have to sacrifice productivity—it actually enhances it. After a night of good sleep, you'll feel more energized, focused, and ready to tackle your tasks with improved efficiency.

Active Rest: More than Just Sleep

Physical rest goes beyond just sleep. Active rest, such as yoga, deep breathing exercises, and mindful movement, plays a vital role in rejuvenating the body. Yoga, for instance, combines controlled movements, stretching, and breathwork to relax the muscles and ease tension, helping the body recover from physical exertion. Regular practice can also improve flexibility, reduce injury risk, and enhance posture, all of which contribute to long-term physical health.

Deep Breathing for Recovery:

Deep breathing exercises, especially diaphragmatic breathing, stimulate the parasympathetic nervous system, which is responsible for rest and digestion. This practice can lower cortisol levels, reduce stress, and enhance oxygen delivery to muscles, aiding in faster recovery. Whether it's through guided meditation or a simple breathing exercise, incorporating deep breathing into your day can have immediate restorative effects on the body.

Nutrition: Fueling the Body for Rest

What we consume directly impacts how well our bodies recover. Proper nutrition is crucial for muscle repair, hormone balance, and energy levels. Athletes like Tom Brady follow strict diets rich in anti-inflammatory foods, lean proteins, and whole grains to fuel their bodies for optimum recovery. Ensuring your diet is balanced and filled with nutrient-dense foods can significantly improve the quality of your physical rest.

Key Foods for Recovery:

Proteins (lean meats, fish, legumes) aid in muscle repair.

Antioxidants (berries, leafy greens) help reduce inflammation.

Magnesium-rich foods (nuts, seeds, dark chocolate) promote relaxation and better sleep quality.

Hydration is another critical factor for physical recovery. Drinking sufficient water helps flush out toxins, transport nutrients, and maintain energy levels throughout the day.

Anecdotes: The Rest Strategies of Top Performers

The world's top athletes know the value of rest. For example, NBA superstar LeBron James is known for investing heavily in his recovery. He spends over a million dollars annually on techniques like cryotherapy, hyperbaric chambers, and massage therapy. LeBron also prioritizes sleep, aiming for 12 hours a day when training heavily. His focus on rest has enabled him to maintain peak performance throughout his 20+ year career.

Similarly, NFL quarterback Tom Brady is famous for his disciplined lifestyle, which includes a heavy emphasis on recovery. Brady follows a strict sleep schedule, aiming for 9 hours of sleep each night, and practices regular yoga and deep breathing to manage stress. His attention to rest and recovery has been a key factor in his ability to compete at an elite level well into his 40s.

These athletes' stories underscore an essential truth: it is not just hard work that leads to success, but strategic rest as well. By prioritizing recovery, they have not only extended their careers but have also consistently performed at the top of their games.

Practical Strategies for Physical Renewal

Prioritize Sleep: Aim for 7-9 hours of quality sleep each night, and maintain a consistent sleep schedule. Create a sleep-friendly environment—keep your room dark, quiet, and cool, and limit screen time before bed.

Incorporate Active Rest: Engage in low-intensity activities such as yoga, stretching, or walking to allow your body to recover without complete inactivity. These exercises also reduce muscle stiffness and improve flexibility.

Practice Deep Breathing: Spend 5-10 minutes each day focusing on deep, diaphragmatic breathing to reduce stress and promote physical recovery.

Eat for Recovery: Prioritize a balanced diet rich in proteins, healthy fats, and antioxidants. Hydrate regularly to help your body detoxify and repair tissues more efficiently.

Listen to Your Body: Recognize when your body is fatigued and needs a break. Overexertion without adequate rest can lead to injuries and long-term damage.

The Power of Rest for Peak Performance

When you embrace the concept of rest as a critical factor for physical renewal, you unlock the full potential of your body. Just like top athletes, we must learn to balance hard work with strategic recovery. Physical rest is not a luxury—it's a necessity for those who wish to perform at their best, whether in sports, business, or life.

By incorporating rest and recovery techniques into your daily routine, you'll not only improve your health but also enhance your energy levels, focus, and productivity. Rest is not the opposite of productivity; it is the key to sustaining it.

CHAPTER 6

REST FOR THE MIND

THE ROLE OF MENTAL BREAKS IN GROWTH

In today's fast-paced world, mental breaks have become a necessity, not a luxury. With the constant flood of information and digital stimuli, our minds are often overwhelmed, leading to fatigue, burnout, and decreased clarity. But by intentionally pausing and resting the mind, we not only preserve our mental health but also set the stage for renewed growth and resilience.

The Overstimulated Mind

From the moment we wake up, we are bombarded with notifications, messages, news, and endless streams of information. This digital overload forces our brains into a state of hyperactivity, leaving little room for quiet reflection or genuine creativity. The more we remain plugged into this continuous flow, the more we drain our cognitive energy, eventually hitting a point of mental exhaustion.

However, the human brain thrives on balance. Just as our bodies need rest after physical exertion, our minds need breaks to recover from intense cognitive work. These mental pauses, when taken deliberately and strategically, offer more than just relief from stress—they provide a critical boost to clarity, creativity, and overall growth.

Mental Breaks as Catalysts for Resilience

Mental resilience is not just the ability to power through challenges; it's the capacity to bounce back, adapt, and evolve in the face of adversity. This resilience is built through the cycle of exertion and rest. When we pause, we allow our brains to consolidate information, process emotions, and foster creative connections that are not possible when we're constantly "on."

In moments of rest, the brain engages in what neuroscientists call the default mode network—a state where the mind drifts, reflects, and makes sense of our experiences. This state is essential for personal growth, problem-solving, and emotional regulation. Without these mental breaks, we miss out on the depth of thought necessary for insight and innovation.

The Power of Disconnecting

Digital devices are often the main culprit behind our overstimulated minds. We've grown so accustomed to checking our phones or scrolling through social media during any lull that true mental rest feels elusive. To counter this, we need to make disconnecting a deliberate practice.

Disconnecting doesn't necessarily mean abandoning technology altogether, but creating boundaries and being mindful of how we use it. Carving out time each day where we step away from screens—whether through mindfulness practices, walks in nature, or even simple moments of stillness—can profoundly impact our mental clarity and emotional well-being.

The beauty of disconnecting lies in its ability to reawaken our senses. It allows us to return to the present moment, to engage with the world around us with fresh eyes, and to tap into deeper layers of thought. This space away from the constant barrage of stimuli fosters creativity, focus, and the kind of mental clarity that fuels long-term growth.

Micro-Practices for Mental Rest

While long vacations or creative retreats are valuable, they are not always practical in our busy lives. Fortunately, mental breaks can be as short as a few minutes, yet still offer immense benefits. These micro-practices, or brief moments of intentional pause, are an excellent way to refresh the mind without disrupting our daily flow.

One powerful tool is the practice of "mindful minutes." These are short, one- to five-minute breaks where we step away from our tasks, close our eyes, and focus on our breath or a calming thought. In these moments, we release the mental clutter, allowing our minds to rest and reset. Mindful minutes can be practiced anywhere—at your desk, during a commute, or even in the middle of a meeting. The goal is to train the brain to pause and rejuvenate, even in high-pressure environments.

Another simple yet effective tool is the "5-4-3-2-1" grounding exercise. This technique involves taking a moment to reconnect with your surroundings through your senses: identify five things you can see, four things you can touch, three things you can hear, two things you can smell, and one thing you can taste. This exercise pulls the mind away from distractions and centers it in the present, providing an immediate mental break.

Creative Retreats: The Deep Pause

While micro-practices offer quick relief, deeper mental rest often requires more immersive experiences. Creative retreats—whether they last a few days or just a weekend—allow the mind to detach from routine and sink into an extended period of rest and reflection. These retreats are an opportunity to step away from the busyness of daily life and focus on activities that nurture the mind and soul.

Creative retreats need not be extravagant or expensive. A simple weekend spent offline, engaged in activities like journaling, painting, or hiking, can have profound effects on mental clarity. The key is to create space for uninterrupted thought, allowing the mind to wander and explore without the constraints of daily obligations.

Growth through Rest

True mental growth is not achieved through constant striving or relentless productivity. It comes from finding balance—between work and rest, stimulation and stillness. By integrating strategic mental breaks into our routines, we cultivate the resilience and clarity needed to navigate life's challenges.

Mental rest is not about idleness; it is an active investment in our well-being. It empowers us to return to our work and our lives with renewed energy, focus, and creativity. In embracing the art of rest, we unlock the full potential of our minds and open ourselves to the limitless possibilities of growth.

CHAPTER 7

REST FOR THE SPIRIT
ALIGNING PURPOSE WITH RESTFUL LIVING

Amid the constant pressure to achieve, produce, and move forward, it's easy to lose sight of our deeper purpose, the driving force behind why we do what we do. But in neglecting spiritual rest, we risk burnout, disconnection, and an overarching sense of meaninglessness. To align with a higher purpose, one must learn to rest purposefully, using moments of stillness to renew the spirit and find balance between achievement and meaning.

The Need for Spiritual Renewal

While physical and mental rest are crucial for rejuvenation, spiritual rest addresses something even more fundamental—the health of the soul. This kind of rest allows individuals to step back from the noise of daily life and realign with their inner values and purpose. It is in moments of quiet introspection, meditation, or religious practice that people often rediscover what truly matters to them.

Spiritual rest involves more than just taking a break from work; it is about creating space to reflect on life's deeper questions: Why am I here? What is my calling? Am I aligned with my purpose? These moments of reflection not only bring clarity but also nurture a sense of fulfillment, helping us to continue pursuing goals with renewed energy and direction.

Incorporating Purposeful Rest

Purposeful rest is not about escaping responsibilities but about recharging the spirit in a way that enhances one's ability to fulfill those responsibilities. Ancient practices such as the Sabbath are examples of this. Traditionally observed as a day of rest, the Sabbath provides a structured period for people to cease their labor, reflect on their spiritual beliefs, and spend time with family and community. This ritual encourages individuals to pause and reconnect with their core values, ultimately leading to a deeper sense of purpose and peace.

Similarly, modern spiritual retreats offer another avenue for aligning purpose with restful living. These retreats, often held in serene environments, invite participants to unplug from their hectic routines and engage in practices like meditation, yoga, or silent reflection. By distancing themselves from everyday stressors, individuals can gain a broader perspective on their life's direction and emerge with a clearer sense of purpose.

Balancing Achievement with Meaning

In the drive to achieve more, people often push

themselves beyond their limits, believing that success lies in constant action. However, without moments of spiritual renewal, this drive can lead to exhaustion, frustration, and a sense of emptiness. Purposeful rest serves as a counterbalance, ensuring that achievement is not hollow but meaningful.

By integrating practices like meditation, prayer, or mindful reflection into daily life, individuals can maintain a balance between striving for external success and nourishing their inner world. When we allow ourselves to rest in alignment with our values, our achievements become expressions of purpose rather than mere results. It is through this balance that we find lasting fulfillment and joy in our pursuits.

Example: Sabbaths and Spiritual Retreats

The concept of the Sabbath, found in many religious traditions, illustrates how rest can be deeply intertwined with purpose. In Judaism, for instance, the Sabbath is a day of rest where work ceases, and time is devoted to worship, reflection, and community. This deliberate pause allows individuals to renew their spiritual energy, reconnect with their beliefs, and refocus their lives on what matters most.

Spiritual retreats, which have gained popularity in recent years, also offer a structured opportunity for spiritual renewal. These retreats often take place in peaceful natural settings and provide a break from the demands of daily life. Participants engage in activities designed to foster introspection, such as meditation, journaling, or walking in nature. By stepping away from the hustle of life, they gain fresh insights into their purpose and often return to their routines with a clearer sense of direction.

Practical Steps for Spiritual Rest

To cultivate rest for the spirit, consider the following practices:

1. Daily Reflection: Set aside time each day for quiet reflection. Whether through journaling, meditation, or prayer, this practice allows you to reconnect with your inner self and evaluate whether your actions are aligned with your values.

2. Sabbaths or Rest Days: Designate one day each week to step away from work and engage in activities that nurture your spirit. Use this time to focus on personal growth, spiritual beliefs, or spending quality time with loved ones.

3. Spiritual Retreats: Consider attending a spiritual retreat or creating your own retreat at home. Dedicate a few days to disconnecting from technology and responsibilities, allowing yourself time to reflect, meditate, and realign with your purpose.

4. Mindful Living: Incorporate mindfulness into your daily activities, whether it's eating, walking, or even working. By remaining present, you bring a sense of purpose and intention to everything you do, creating moments of spiritual renewal even in the midst of a busy day.

Conclusion: Rising Through Rest

Rest for the spirit is not a luxury but a necessity. By aligning restful living with a sense of purpose, we can create a life that balances achievement with meaning. Purposeful rest, whether through daily reflection, religious observances, or retreats, allows us to reconnect with our deepest values and emerge renewed, ready to face life's challenges with clarity and strength. In this way, rest becomes the foundation upon which we build a life of true success and fulfillment.

CHAPTER 8

HIBERNATION VS HUSTLE
REFRAMING PRODUCTIVITY IN THEMODERN WORLD

The rise of "hustle culture" has further ingrained the idea that rest is a weakness and that the road to success is paved with endless hours of labor, often at the expense of personal well-being. But what if the key to sustainable success is not found in constant hustle, but in intentional rest? This chapter challenges the myth of perpetual work and highlights the power of strategic hibernation—embracing periods of rest to achieve long-term productivity and fulfillment.

The Myth of Hustle Culture

Hustle culture glorifies busyness. It tells us that the more we work, the more we will achieve, and that success is reserved for those willing to sacrifice sleep, leisure, and even relationships. This mindset has led to a societal epidemic of burnout, where people find themselves exhausted, disengaged, and often struggling to maintain their health or happiness.

The reality is that while hustle may yield short-term results, it is unsustainable in the long run. The body, mind, and spirit require periods of rest to recharge, innovate, and perform optimally. When rest is neglected, productivity eventually plummets, and the quality of work suffers. Worse, without sufficient recovery time, individuals are more prone to stress-related illnesses, anxiety, and burnout.

Reframing Productivity: The Power of Hibernation

In contrast to hustle culture, the concept of hibernation offers a healthier and more strategic approach to productivity. Just as animals retreat during winter to conserve energy and ensure their survival, people can adopt periods of rest as a way to recharge and prepare for the next phase of growth. This "strategic hibernation" allows individuals to pause, reflect, and regenerate, leading to more creative, focused, and sustainable output when they return to their work.

The key insight here is that productivity is not simply about how many hours are worked but how effectively those hours are spent. Hibernation encourages deliberate rest, which leads to greater clarity, enhanced problem-solving skills, and deeper insights—qualities that constant hustle fails to nurture.

Why Hibernation Works?

Research supports the idea that rest is essential for optimal performance. Studies on sleep and productivity reveal that well-rested individuals outperform their sleep-deprived counterparts in terms of creativity, decision-making, and problem-solving. Neuroscientists have found that periods of rest, particularly deep rest such as sleep or meditation, allow the brain to process information, make connections, and generate new ideas.

In contrast, those who subscribe to the hustle mentality often find themselves mentally fatigued, unable to innovate, and stuck in a cycle of diminishing returns. The long-term benefits of strategic rest far outweigh the temporary gains of working without pause. Rest allows for recovery, renewal, and the development of a deeper sense of purpose, which are crucial for sustained productivity.

Case Study: Companies Embracing Work-Rest Balance

While hustle culture may dominate certain industries, forward-thinking companies are starting to recognize the value of balancing work with rest. These companies understand that employees who are well-rested and mentally refreshed are more productive, creative, and loyal. Here are a few examples of organizations that have successfully integrated rest into their work culture:

1. Google's Nap Pods

Google, one of the most innovative companies in the world, is known for its unique approach to workplace productivity. At their headquarters,

Google has installed nap pods, specially designed sleeping stations where employees can take short naps during the workday. The idea behind this is simple: short, strategic naps boost cognitive function, enhance creativity, and improve overall performance.

By encouraging employees to rest when they need it, Google has fostered an environment where innovation thrives. The company understands that creativity and problem-solving cannot flourish in a state of exhaustion, and they have designed their workspaces to promote a balance of focused work and rest.

2. Scandinavia's Shorter Workweeks

Scandinavian countries, particularly Sweden and Denmark, have long been proponents of shorter workweeks and more generous vacation time. In Sweden, for instance, some companies have experimented with six-hour workdays without sacrificing productivity. The results have been impressive: employees report higher levels of job satisfaction, less stress, and greater work-life balance. Surprisingly, companies also found that productivity did not decrease—in some cases, it even increased.

This model challenges the traditional notion that more work hours translate to greater output. Instead, it demonstrates that by working fewer hours and allowing time for rest and personal fulfillment, employees can achieve the same or even better results.

3. Basecamp's Emphasis on Work-Life Balance

Basecamp, a software company, has built its entire culture around the principle of work-life balance. The company discourages long work hours and overtime, insisting that employees prioritize rest and personal time. Basecamp's leadership believes that creativity and productivity come from a place of mental and emotional well-being, which is only possible when work does not dominate every aspect of life.

By valuing rest, Basecamp has cultivated a workforce that is both highly productive and deeply engaged. Employees are encouraged to take regular breaks, disconnect from work outside office hours, and spend time pursuing personal interests. This holistic approach to productivity stands in stark contrast to the hustle-driven environments found in many other tech companies.

4. Infosys: Quiet Rooms for Meditation

Infosys, a global leader in technology services and consulting, has recognized the tv importance of employee well-being and mental health in boosting productivity. The company has implemented "quiet rooms" across its campuses in India, where employees can take breaks for meditation, reflection, or simply unwind in a peaceful environment. These rooms are designed to provide employees with a moment of calm amid the hustle, promoting mindfulness and mental clarity, which can significantly improve focus and decision-making.

Infosys understands that sustained productivity is not a result of constant work but a balance between focused effort and mental rejuvenation. By promoting practices like meditation, Infosys encourages its employees to take mindful breaks, enhancing their creativity, reducing stress, and preventing burnout.

5. Tata Consultancy Services (TCS): Flexible Work Culture and Wellness Programs

Tata Consultancy Services (TCS), one of India's largest IT services companies, has long been a pioneer in creating a healthy work environment that values rest and well-being. TCS offers flexible working hours and remote work options, allowing employees to balance their professional responsibilities with personal well-being. The company has also integrated wellness programs such as yoga, health check-ups, and stress management workshops into its employee care initiatives.

TCS believes that a flexible, well-balanced work schedule allows employees to maintain their productivity without sacrificing their health. By encouraging a healthy work-life balance, TCS has not only improved employee satisfaction but also increased long-term productivity and engagement.

These Indian companies, like Google, are proving that rest and rejuvenation are essential components of modern productivity. By prioritizing the well-being of their employees, they are fostering an environment where creativity, innovation, and sustained success can thrive.

The Long-Term Benefits of Rest over Burnout

The lesson from companies like Google, Scandinavian organizations, and Basecamp is clear: rest is not a barrier to success but a catalyst for it. In fact, periods of rest can lead to more sustainable and impactful outcomes than prolonged hustle ever could.

When individuals prioritize rest, they give themselves the opportunity to replenish their energy, reconnect with their values, and gain a broader perspective on their goals. This ultimately allows them to return to their work with renewed focus and creativity. In contrast, burnout caused by constant hustle diminishes long-term productivity, leading to decreased motivation, poor health, and high turnover in companies.

Strategic hibernation, whether in the form of naps, shorter workweeks, or time away from the office, is a practice that acknowledges the natural rhythms of human performance. Just as nature has cycles of activity and dormancy, so too should our approach to work. By allowing time for rest and renewal, we can rise to greater heights of success and satisfaction.

Conclusion: A New Approach to Success

It's time to rethink the way we approach productivity. The hustle culture that dominates modern workspaces is not the only—or even the best—path to success. Instead, we must embrace the idea that rest, particularly strategic hibernation, is a crucial component of long-term achievement. By balancing work with periods of rest, we can avoid burnout, enhance creativity, and achieve a more meaningful and sustainable form of success.

Hibernation is not about laziness or avoiding hard work; it is about working smarter, not harder. It is about recognizing that rest is not a luxury but a necessity for rising to our fullest potential. As more individuals and organizations adopt this mindset, we may finally move beyond the myth of hustle and embrace a healthier, more balanced approach to success.

CHAPTER 9

THE POWER OF THE PAUSE
STRATEGIC BREAKS FOR BREAKTHROUGHS

History has repeatedly shown that some of the greatest breakthroughs—whether for individuals or organizations—come after strategic pauses. Far from being a moment of inaction, these breaks serve as opportunities for reflection, reinvention, and renewal. Pausing is not about stopping; it's about preparing for a stronger, more focused comeback.

The Purpose of Pausing

The power of a pause lies in its ability to create space. This space allows for introspection, creative thinking, and the realignment of purpose. While constant motion can lead to burnout or blind adherence to old ways of doing things, a well-timed pause disrupts this momentum and offers a fresh perspective.

Pauses can be intentional, like taking a sabbatical or strategic break, or they can come as a result of external forces, such as a recession or a global crisis. In either case, what happens during the pause often determines the success of what follows. Whether it's an individual seeking personal growth or a company looking for innovation, strategic breaks have repeatedly proven to be the foundation of significant breakthroughs.

Case Study: Steve Jobs' Return to Apple

One of the most famous examples of a strategic pause leading to massive breakthroughs is Steve Jobs' return to Apple. After being ousted from the company he co-founded in 1985, Jobs took a step back, and while it may have seemed like the end of his career at Apple, it was only the beginning of something bigger.

During his time away from Apple, Jobs founded NeXT, a company that, while not a commercial success, was crucial in his development as a leader and visionary. He also acquired Pixar, which became a groundbreaking force in animation. These ventures allowed Jobs to explore new ideas, develop fresh approaches to leadership, and gain invaluable experience.

When Jobs returned to Apple in 1997, the company was on the brink of bankruptcy. However, armed with the lessons learned during his time away, Jobs led the company through one of the most remarkable corporate turnarounds in history. Apple didn't just survive—it became one of the most valuable and innovative companies in the world. The iMac, iPod, iPhone, and iPad were all products of the innovation that stemmed from Jobs' strategic pause.

Jobs' time away from Apple highlights an essential truth: pausing can be a time to gather strength, reflect on mistakes, and return with renewed clarity and focus.

The Corporate Pause: Innovation in Times of Recession

Organizations, too, can benefit from strategic pauses, especially during times of crisis or recession. While some companies panic and slash innovation efforts during economic downturns, others use these moments as opportunities to rethink their strategies, innovate, and prepare for the future.

Take, for instance, companies like Netflix and Airbnb, both of which made crucial decisions during economic recessions that led to significant breakthroughs.

Netflix: In the early 2000s, Netflix was primarily a DVD rental service competing with Blockbuster. The dot-com bubble burst in 2001, and many tech companies collapsed, but Netflix used this economic downturn as an opportunity to pivot. They began investing in a streaming model and later original content, positioning themselves as leaders in the digital entertainment space. By the time the Great Recession hit in 2008, Netflix had already established itself as a household name, offering affordable entertainment at a time when many people were cutting back on expenses. Their decision to innovate during the pause of an economic downturn became the foundation of their future success.

Zomato: Navigating the 2020 Pandemic

Zomato, India's leading food delivery platform, experienced a massive disruption during the COVID-19 pandemic in 2020, with restaurants shutting down and demand for food delivery dropping. Instead of panicking, Zomato used this pause to reassess its business model and innovate. The company quickly pivoted to offer grocery delivery services under Zomato Market, meeting the growing demand for essentials during lockdowns.

Additionally, Zomato invested heavily in safety protocols for food delivery, building trust with customers during uncertain times. This innovation and adaptation during a period of crisis helped Zomato recover faster than many competitors. By the time the economy started reopening, Zomato had strengthened its position in the market, eventually leading to its successful IPO in 2021, making it one of India's first tech unicorns to go public.

OYO Rooms: Thriving Post-Demonetization

Founded in 2013, OYO Rooms faced significant challenges during the Indian government's demonetization policy in 2016, which affected the entire hospitality sector due to reduced cash flow and consumer spending. However, rather than retracting, OYO used this period of economic pause to rethink and refine its business model.

OYO shifted its focus from a cash-heavy operation to online payments and digital-first solutions, catering to the changing landscape. They also leveraged technology to offer better standardized hotel services and expanded globally during this time. By innovating during an economic downturn, OYO emerged as a leader in budget accommodation, scaling operations internationally across multiple markets.

Airbnb: Founded in 2008 during the global financial crisis, Airbnb emerged from a period of economic uncertainty. The founders recognized that, with many people struggling financially, there was an opportunity for everyday individuals to rent out their spare rooms to generate extra income. Rather than waiting for the economy to recover, Airbnb capitalized on the financial challenges people were facing and built a business model that thrived in the wake of the recession. Today, Airbnb is one of the world's largest accommodation providers, despite owning no real estate themselves.

These examples show that recessions and downturns can be strategic pauses for innovation rather than periods of decline. Companies that approach these times as opportunities for reinvention often come out stronger on the other side.

Personal Renewal: The Impact of Sabbaticals Individuals, like organizations, can experience significant breakthroughs when they step away from their routine and allow themselves time to rest and reflect. Sabbaticals—extended breaks from work or daily responsibilities—have been used by many successful individuals to recharge their creative and mental energies.

Bill Gates: Every year, Bill Gates takes a "Think Week"—a retreat where he spends time alone reading, thinking, and brainstorming new ideas. It was during one of these breaks that Gates came up with the idea for Microsoft's Internet Explorer, which became a crucial component of the company's success in the early days of the internet. By stepping away from the day-to-day demands of running Microsoft, Gates was able to view the larger picture and focus on long-term innovation.

Sheryl Sandberg: The COO of Facebook and author of Lean In, Sheryl Sandberg, took a personal pause after the sudden death of her husband in 2015. During this time, she not only grieved but also reflected on her own life, work, and priorities. This period of introspection led to her writing the book Option B, where she explored resilience and personal growth in the face of adversity. The lessons she learned during her personal pause profoundly shaped her approach to leadership and life.

The Benefits of Pausing

The key benefit of strategic pauses—whether for individuals or organizations—is the clarity they provide. When you step back from the noise and chaos of everyday life, you gain a broader perspective. Problems that once seemed insurmountable become more manageable, and new ideas that were previously obscured by busyness have the chance to emerge.

Here are some of the long-term benefits of incorporating pauses into your life or organization:

1. **Creative Breakthroughs:** Pauses create mental space, allowing for the incubation of ideas. Many of the world's greatest inventions and innovations were born during periods of rest or reflection.

2. **Personal and Professional Growth:** Stepping back gives individuals the chance to evaluate their goals, values, and priorities. Sabbaticals or retreats can lead to significant personal development, new insights, and more meaningful contributions when they return to work.

3. **Prevention of Burnout:** Pausing prevents burnout by allowing time for rest and recovery. It also promotes mental clarity, emotional well-being, and physical health, ensuring long-term productivity.

4. Strategic Innovation: For companies, strategic pauses—whether during recessions or planned breaks—offer the chance to rethink business models, innovate, and adapt to changing markets.

Conclusion: Embracing the Power of the Pause

The lesson is clear: pausing is not about giving up or stopping; it's about preparing for a stronger comeback. By embracing strategic breaks, individuals and organizations can create space for reflection, innovation, and personal renewal. Whether it's taking a sabbatical, retreating for a "Think Week," or navigating a corporate pause during a recession, the power of the pause can lead to breakthroughs that far exceed the results of continuous hustle.

The next time you feel stuck, overwhelmed, or unsure of your direction, consider taking a pause. Step back, reflect, and allow your mind and spirit to recharge. What you'll find is that sometimes, the greatest progress comes from moments of stillness. In the quiet of the pause, the seeds of your next breakthrough are often quietly waiting to grow.

CHAPTER 10

REST AS A FORM OF RESISTANCE
PUSHING BACK AGAINST BURNOUT

Society encourages us to measure our worth by how much we can accomplish, how fast we can work, and how seamlessly we can juggle multiple roles. This pressure to always be "on" has led to a burnout epidemic—where exhaustion, stress, and disengagement have become all too common. But what if rest could be our form of resistance? What if, instead of succumbing to the societal pressure to constantly hustle, we could reclaim rest as an essential act of self-care and rebellion against burnout?

In this chapter, we will explore how rest, far from being a luxury or sign of laziness, is a radical act of self-preservation in a world that demands perpetual productivity. By prioritizing rest, we push back against the culture of burnout and reclaim our well-being and sense of purpose.

The Culture of Burnout

The term "burnout" was first coined in the 1970s to describe the emotional and physical exhaustion that caregivers experienced due to chronic stress. Today, burnout is no longer confined to a specific profession or demographic; it has become a widespread issue, affecting workers across all fields. The constant pressure to meet deadlines, stay connected, and achieve more in less time has led to a generation of people who are burned out, both mentally and physically.

At its core, burnout is the result of prolonged, unmanaged stress. It manifests in feelings of overwhelming fatigue, cynicism about work, and a sense of ineffectiveness. The World Health Organization has even recognized burnout as a serious occupational phenomenon. Yet, despite this growing awareness, many people still feel trapped by the relentless demands of work.

But what if we challenged this narrative? What if rest, instead of hustle, became our badge of honor? By reframing rest as an intentional, purposeful act, we can begin to shift the conversation around productivity and success.

Rest as Resistance

Rest is not a sign of weakness—it is an act of defiance against a society that equates busyness with value. In a culture where being overworked is celebrated, rest becomes a radical form of self-care. By choosing to rest, we resist the notion that our worth is tied to how much we can produce. We reject the idea that being constantly busy is a virtue and instead embrace the truth that we are worthy of care, attention, and renewal.

Rest allows us to step away from the grind and reconnect with ourselves. It gives us the space to reflect, breathe, and nurture our physical, mental, and emotional health. In choosing to rest, we claim ownership of our time, energy, and well-being.

The late activist and scholar Audre Lorde famously said, "Caring for myself is not self-indulgence, it is self-preservation, and that is an act of political warfare." For Lorde, taking time for oneself was an act of survival in a society that often devalues marginalized voices. In a similar vein, rest can be seen as a form of resistance against a system that prioritizes profits over people.

Stories of Burnout and Recovery

The power of rest as resistance becomes clear when we look at the stories of those who have reached the brink of burnout and found their way back through the power of rest. These individuals did not just take a break; they used rest as a tool to realign their priorities, reshape their relationship with work, and ultimately transform their lives.

Neha's Story: Redefining Success

Neha, a high-achieving corporate lawyer, was the embodiment of hustle culture. Working 60- to 70-hour weeks, she prided herself on her ability to juggle countless tasks and still deliver top results. But after years of relentless work, Neha found herself physically and emotionally drained. She began to experience chronic fatigue, anxiety, and a growing sense of dissatisfaction with her career. Despite outward success, she felt disconnected from her own life.

Eventually, Neha hit a breaking point. After a particularly grueling project, she collapsed from exhaustion and was forced to take time off. During this break, Neha realized that her constant need to achieve had come at the expense of her health and happiness. She began practicing mindfulness, engaging in hobbies she had long abandoned, and reconnecting with loved ones.

Through this process, Neha discovered that rest was not the opposite of success—it was essential to it. She returned to work with a new perspective, setting clear boundaries and prioritizing her well-being. Neha's experience taught her that true success is not measured by how much we accomplish but by how well we take care of ourselves in the process.

Anurag's Story: The Power of Stepping Away

Anurag was a startup founder who thrived on the thrill of entrepreneurship. He worked around the clock, fueled by a belief that success required relentless effort. However, the pressure to grow his business led to overwhelming stress. As deadlines piled up and expectations grew, Anurag found himself on the edge of burnout.

One day, after an intense bout of insomnia and panic attacks, Anurag made a radical decision: he would take a full month off to rest and recharge. At first, the idea seemed impossible. How could he leave his business for that long? But as the days passed, Anurag realized that stepping away gave him a much-needed break to reflect on the direction of his company.

During his month of rest, Anurag reconnected with his creative side. He began reading, traveling, and spending time in nature. This time away allowed him to gain new insights into his business, and when he returned, he implemented changes that ultimately improved both his personal life and the company's success.

Anurag's story is a testament to the power of rest as a transformative force. It was through taking a step back that he was able to find the clarity and creativity needed to move forward.

Reclaiming Well-being in a Work-Obsessed World
The stories of Neha and Anurag show that rest is not merely a break from work; it is a critical component of a balanced and meaningful life. In pushing back against burnout, rest becomes a tool for reclaiming well-being, both physically and emotionally.

Here are some practical steps to incorporate rest as a form of resistance in your own life:

1. Set Boundaries: Establish clear boundaries between work and personal life. Prioritize rest by scheduling breaks, time off, and activities that rejuvenate your mind and body.

2. Listen to Your Body: Pay attention to the signs of burnout, such as fatigue, irritability, or loss of motivation. When your body signals the need for rest, honor it.

3. Unplug: In today's digital age, we are always connected. Make a conscious effort to unplug from work emails, social media, and other distractions during your rest time. Create a space where rest can thrive without the noise of constant communication.

4. Normalize Rest: Advocate for a culture that values rest. In the workplace, encourage conversations around the importance of taking breaks, and lead by example. In your personal life, support those around you in their pursuit of balance and well-being.

Conclusion: The Quiet Revolution of Rest

Rest is a powerful, often overlooked form of resistance. It challenges the societal norms that glorify overwork and reminds us that our worth is not determined by our productivity. By choosing rest, we choose to prioritize our well-being, creativity, and inner peace over the demands of a burnout-driven culture.

In the quiet moments of rest, we find space to breathe, reflect, and reconnect with ourselves. We reclaim control of our time, and in doing so, we rise stronger, more centered, and more resilient. In the hustle-driven world we live in, rest is not only a form of self-care—it's a revolutionary act.

CHAPTER 11

CREATIVE HIBERNATION
UNLEASHING INNOVATION THROUGH STILLNESS

Creativity thrives in the spaces where the mind is free to wander, untethered from deadlines and pressure. This is the essence of creative hibernation—the practice of using purposeful rest to nurture innovation and problem-solving.

In this chapter, we explore how stillness and detachment can unlock the most creative parts of our minds, allowing us to approach challenges with fresh perspectives. We will also look at how some of the greatest minds in history—artists, scientists, and thinkers—embraced rest as a powerful tool to unleash their creative potential.

The Myth of Constant Creativity

There is a pervasive myth that creativity demands constant engagement, that in order to generate great ideas, we must always be working on something, always thinking, always creating. But this couldn't be further from the truth. Research shows that our brains need time to rest, to disengage, in order to process and connect ideas in new ways. In fact, studies on the brain's "default mode network" reveal that when we are in a relaxed state—daydreaming, meditating, or simply taking a walk—

our minds are still hard at work behind the scenes, making the connections that lead to creative breakthroughs.

The idea that rest fuels creativity is not new. From artists and musicians to scientists and inventors, some of history's greatest minds understood that true creativity often requires stepping away from the grind, allowing the mind to roam freely. By embracing rest, we invite innovation.

The Role of Downtime in Creative Breakthroughs

When we think of great inventions, works of art, or musical compositions, we often imagine their creators working tirelessly to achieve perfection. Yet, many of these great accomplishments were born in moments of rest or detachment from the task at hand. Creative hibernation provides the space for ideas to incubate, allowing the subconscious mind to work on problems in ways that the conscious mind cannot.

Leonardo da Vinci: The Power of Pausing

Leonardo da Vinci, one of the greatest creative geniuses in history, was known for taking long breaks from his projects. Da Vinci believed that stepping away from his work allowed him to see things from a new perspective. His notebooks are filled with ideas that seem to have emerged during periods of rest or wandering. For da Vinci, these moments of creative hibernation were essential for refining his innovations, from his paintings to his scientific discoveries.

One of his most famous works, the Mona Lisa, took years to complete, not because of a lack of effort, but because da Vinci allowed the painting to evolve over time. By taking extended pauses, he could return to the piece with fresh insights and inspiration. Da Vinci's approach to creativity—one of patience and purposeful rest—demonstrates the importance of allowing ideas to breathe before reaching their full potential.

Rabindranath Tagore: The Power of Solitude

Rabindranath Tagore, India's Nobel laureate in literature, believed deeply in the power of solitude to fuel his creativity. Known for his poetry, songs, and philosophical writings, Tagore often retreated to his family estate in Shantiniketan, where he would spend long hours alone in nature. These periods of creative hibernation were vital to his creative process. Tagore's works, like Gitanjali (for which he received the Nobel Prize), were often born out of moments of reflection and calm, where he allowed his thoughts to flow freely.

Tagore's creativity thrived in these tranquil periods, when he was able to detach from the demands of society and immerse himself in the rhythms of nature. His ability to produce groundbreaking literary and artistic work, even at times of national turmoil, is a testament to the importance of stillness in unlocking innovation.

Srinivasa Ramanujan: Insights in Dreamlike States

Srinivasa Ramanujan, the self-taught mathematical genius from India, provides another example of how creativity can be unleashed through moments of stillness. Ramanujan often claimed that many of his most profound mathematical discoveries came to him in dreams. He described receiving mathematical formulas from the Hindu goddess Namagiri during his dreams and periods of deep contemplation. These moments of detachment, when his mind wandered freely, allowed him to tap into a vast creative reservoir.

Though he lacked formal training, Ramanujan's ability to connect seemingly disparate ideas during moments of reflection and rest led to some of the most important contributions to number theory and mathematical analysis. His story demonstrates how stillness and creative hibernation can lead to breakthroughs that defy conventional wisdom, even in highly analytical fields.

Pyotr Ilyich Tchaikovsky: Composing Through Stillness

The great Russian composer Pyotr Ilyich Tchaikovsky was another advocate of rest as a means of fostering creativity. Though he is known for his dramatic and powerful compositions, Tchaikovsky was deeply attuned to the rhythms of nature and took daily walks to clear his mind. He believed that these periods of stillness and detachment from his work allowed him to channel his creativity more effectively.

Tchaikovsky's creative process involved alternating between intense work sessions and extended breaks. He often described how his best ideas would come to him during these moments of quiet, as if the music flowed to him when his mind was free from pressure. His story reminds us that sometimes the most powerful creative breakthroughs happen when we stop trying so hard and simply let the ideas come.

The Neuroscience of Creative Rest

Modern science supports the idea that rest enhances creativity. When we engage in activities that allow the brain to rest—whether that's sleep, meditation, or simply daydreaming—the brain continues to process information at a deep level. This is when the brain's "default mode network" is most active, working behind the scenes to make new connections between ideas and experiences.

Creative hibernation taps into this natural process. By stepping away from our work, we give our brains the freedom to explore ideas in ways that might not be possible when we are actively engaged. This is why so many people report having "eureka" moments while doing something completely unrelated to their problem, like taking a shower or going for a walk. The act of resting allows the mind to synthesize information in surprising ways, leading to moments of clarity and innovation.

Strategic Breaks for Creative Gains

Incorporating creative hibernation into your routine doesn't mean abandoning hard work. Rather, it's about balancing periods of focused effort with strategic breaks. Here are some ways to harness the power of rest to enhance creativity:

1. Embrace the Power of Daydreaming: Allow yourself to daydream without guilt. This can be a powerful tool for unlocking new ideas. Research has shown that mind-wandering activates parts of the brain associated with creative thinking.

2. Take Walks to Clear Your Mind: Many great thinkers, from Charles Darwin to Steve Jobs, have sworn by the creative benefits of walking. The act of walking, especially in nature, helps the mind relax and can lead to creative breakthroughs.

3. Practice Mindfulness and Meditation: Meditation is a powerful way to quiet the mind and create space for new ideas to emerge. By focusing on the present moment, you clear away mental clutter and open yourself to insights that might otherwise be missed.

4. Allow for Downtime in Your Schedule: Whether it's a long weekend, a vacation, or just an afternoon off, giving yourself time to recharge is essential for creativity. The best ideas often come when we least expect them, so make sure to build periods of rest into your schedule.
5. Sleep on It: Sleep is one of the most effective forms of creative hibernation. Studies show that sleep enhances memory consolidation and problem-solving. When faced with a difficult problem, sometimes the best thing you can do is take a break, get some rest, and return to it with a fresh mind.

Companies That Embrace Creative Hibernation

Forward-thinking companies have begun to realize the value of rest for fostering innovation. Tech giants like Google and Facebook have introduced nap pods and relaxation spaces in their offices to encourage employees to take short breaks throughout the day. The results speak for themselves: employees report feeling more refreshed, creative, and productive after these moments of rest.

In Scandinavia, companies have adopted shorter workweeks, recognizing that well-rested employees are more engaged and innovative. These companies understand that creativity cannot be forced—it requires a balance of work and rest. By encouraging employees to take time off, whether through sabbaticals or simply by leaving the office on time, they are creating an environment where innovation can flourish.

Conclusion: Innovation in Stillness

Creative hibernation is not about avoiding work—it's about working smarter, not harder. The most innovative ideas often come when we are not actively seeking them. By embracing periods of rest, we allow our minds to make new connections, solve problems, and see the world from a fresh perspective.

In a culture that values constant productivity, it can be difficult to justify taking time to rest. But as history has shown us, some of the greatest creative minds understood the power of stillness. Whether it's through daydreaming, walking, or simply stepping away from a project, creative hibernation is a vital part of the innovation process.

When we stop pushing and allow ourselves to pause, we open the door to breakthroughs that we never imagined possible.

CHAPTER 12

THE ART OF DOING NOTHING
EMBRACING STILLNESS FOR GROWTH

We live in an age where busyness is a badge of honor, and idle moments are filled with distractions—checking our phones, scrolling through social media, or finding ways to stay occupied. But there is an art to doing nothing, a practice that can foster personal growth, self-discovery, and profound insight.

This chapter explores the surprising power of stillness and how embracing moments of intentional inactivity can lead to transformative growth. While society pushes us to always be doing, achieving, and moving forward, the greatest breakthroughs often come when we pause, reflect, and allow ourselves the luxury of simply being.

Stillness as a Path to Insight

Many of us are afraid of stillness. We fear that by doing nothing, we are wasting time or losing our competitive edge. But in reality, stillness is not the absence of activity; it is the space in which our minds and hearts can process, reflect, and gain clarity. When we stop rushing, we open ourselves to deeper insights about who we are, what we want, and what truly matters.

In ancient philosophies, the concept of stillness has long been revered. The Taoist idea of wu wei, often translated as "non-doing" or "effortless action," teaches that the most effective way to live is by aligning with the natural flow of life rather than forcing outcomes. Similarly, in many spiritual traditions, moments of silence and solitude are seen as essential for cultivating wisdom and inner peace. By intentionally practicing the art of doing nothing, we create the conditions for profound self-reflection and growth.

The Modern Addiction to Busyness

Our culture glorifies the hustle. We've been conditioned to believe that constant motion—working harder, doing more, filling every minute—is the path to success and fulfillment. Yet, studies show that this relentless pursuit of productivity often leads to burnout, stress, and a sense of disconnection from ourselves.

Many people equate rest with laziness, seeing downtime as unproductive or indulgent. But in truth, rest and stillness are vital components of personal growth. By giving ourselves permission to stop, we create space for self-exploration and healing. In these moments of nothingness, we can listen to our inner voice, process our emotions, and gain perspective on our lives.

The Power of Reflection

One of the greatest gifts of stillness is the opportunity it provides for reflection. When we are constantly in motion, we rarely have the chance to step back and evaluate our choices, our values, and our direction in life. It is in moments of quiet that we can truly assess what is working and what is not. This kind of reflection allows us to make more intentional decisions and to align our actions with our deepest desires and purposes.

Consider the practice of journaling, which has been shown to enhance self-awareness and emotional clarity. When we take the time to reflect on our thoughts, feelings, and experiences, we gain insight into patterns and behaviors that may be holding us back. Similarly, meditation and mindfulness practices encourage us to observe our inner world without judgment, leading to greater understanding and self-compassion.

In this way, stillness becomes a powerful tool for growth. By regularly stepping away from the noise and demands of daily life, we can reconnect with our true selves and cultivate a sense of inner peace and purpose.

Case Study: The Beauty of Boredom

Some of the most creative and successful individuals throughout history have embraced periods of boredom or inactivity as essential to their personal and professional growth. For example, J.K. Rowling came up with the idea for Harry Potter while stuck on a delayed train, allowing her mind to wander without distraction. Steve Jobs often spoke about how stepping away from work allowed him to return with renewed creativity and focus.

Boredom, often seen as a negative state, can actually be a gateway to deeper thinking. When we are not constantly bombarded with stimuli, our minds begin to wander, and in this wandering, we make connections that might not have been possible in a state of busyness. Studies have shown that people are more likely to come up with creative solutions to problems after experiencing periods of boredom.

By embracing moments of boredom or doing nothing, we allow our minds the freedom to explore new ideas and perspectives. It is in these moments that true innovation and personal growth can occur.

The Fear of Stillness

For many, the idea of doing nothing is terrifying. It forces us to confront our thoughts, fears, and uncertainties. When we are busy, we can distract ourselves from the deeper questions that often arise in quiet moments: Am I living a life that aligns with my values? Am I truly happy? What changes do I need to make to feel more fulfilled?

While these questions can be uncomfortable, they are essential for personal growth. Stillness gives us the space to explore them without the distractions of daily life. By facing these questions head-on, we can begin to make meaningful changes that lead to a more authentic and fulfilling life.

Embracing Stillness for Growth: An Exercise

To fully experience the benefits of stillness, I encourage you to take a day—or even just a few hours—of complete rest and reflection. This is not a time to catch up on chores or plan your next steps, but rather an opportunity to simply be with yourself. Here's how to approach this exercise:

1. Create Space: Choose a day or a time when you can be free from obligations. Turn off your phone, avoid distractions, and commit to this time for yourself.

2. Do Nothing: Resist the urge to fill your time with activities. Instead, embrace the art of doing nothing. You might sit in a park, lie down, or simply stare out the window. Let your mind wander without any specific goal.

3. Reflect: After a period of stillness, take some time to reflect. What thoughts or feelings came up during your rest? Did you gain any insights about yourself or your life? You can write down your reflections in a journal if you find that helpful.

4. Practice Mindfulness: Use this time to be fully present. Notice the sounds, sensations, and feelings that arise. If your mind starts to wander, gently bring it back to the present moment.

5. Embrace Boredom: Allow yourself to experience boredom without judgment. See it as a gateway to deeper reflection and creativity.

By intentionally practicing stillness, you can reconnect with your inner self and create the space for personal growth and transformation.

Conclusion: Finding Growth in Stillness

In a world that constantly demands more from us, the art of doing nothing is an act of self-care, an opportunity to nurture our inner lives. Stillness fosters reflection, insight, and growth in ways that busyness never can. When we give ourselves permission to rest, we allow ourselves to grow, not just in our careers or achievements, but in our understanding of who we are and what truly matters.

Embrace the power of stillness and discover the profound growth that comes from simply being. It is in these quiet moments that we find clarity, purpose, and the strength to rise.

CHAPTER 13

RISING STRONG
HOW STRATEGIC REST LEADS TO GREATER ACHIEVEMENT

Rest is often misunderstood. In a society obsessed with hustle and constant productivity, many see rest as a form of weakness, a pause that slows us down. But true rest is far from passive—it is a deliberate, strategic choice that enables us to rise stronger, more focused, and more capable than before. This chapter explores how periods of rest, reflection, and renewal empower people to return to their pursuits with greater energy, clarity, and purpose.

Rest as a Catalyst for Growth

We tend to view achievement as a linear progression—an unbroken chain of effort leading us to success. But in reality, life is cyclical. Growth, whether personal or professional, often follows a pattern of action, rest, reflection, and then renewed action. It is during the times of rest that we gain the insight, energy, and resilience needed for the next phase of our journey.

Consider the natural world. Seasons of growth are followed by periods of dormancy. Trees, for example, shed their leaves and conserve their energy during winter, preparing for the burst of new life in spring. This pattern is mirrored in human achievement. When we allow ourselves to rest and reflect, we are not stepping away from our goals; we are preparing for a stronger ascent.

The Power of Reflection and Clarity

One of the greatest gifts of strategic rest is the clarity it brings. In the hustle and bustle of everyday life, it's easy to lose sight of our true purpose. We become so caught up in the demands of the moment that we forget why we started in the first place. Rest offers a chance to step back, to assess where we are and where we want to go.

Take the example of Viktor Frankl, the renowned psychiatrist and Holocaust survivor. After enduring unimaginable suffering during World War II, Frankl used a period of reflection and rest to develop his groundbreaking work on finding meaning in life, which he later published in Man's Search for Meaning. Frankl's ability to rise strong after such a profound period of suffering is a testament to the power of rest and reflection. He emerged from that dark period not only with personal clarity but with insights that have inspired millions.

Rest as Preparation for Renewal

Rest is not simply about recuperating from exhaustion; it's about rejuvenation. It's the pause that allows us to gather strength and refocus our efforts with renewed vigor. This period of renewal is essential for maintaining long-term productivity and avoiding burnout. Strategic rest helps us align our actions with our purpose, ensuring that when we return to work, we do so with greater intention and effectiveness.

Consider athletes. Professional sports teams and elite athletes understand the critical importance of rest and recovery in achieving peak performance. It is during rest periods that muscles repair, energy is restored, and mental focus is recalibrated. Without these periods of recovery, athletes would quickly burn out and their performance would suffer. The same principle applies to all of us, whether we're working in an office, running a business, or pursuing personal goals.

One example is the story of Arianna Huffington, founder of The Huffington Post. After collapsing from exhaustion in 2007, Huffington re-evaluated her approach to work and rest. She made rest and well-being a priority, not just for herself but for her entire organization. This shift in perspective allowed her to rise stronger, building a media empire that emphasized the importance of balance and well-being in achieving success.

Rising from the Ashes: Stories of Renewal

There are countless stories of individuals who have achieved their greatest successes after periods of rest and reflection. These stories serve as a reminder that rest is not the end of the journey—it is the preparation for a stronger ascent.

Consider the story of Steve Jobs, who was famously ousted from Apple, the company he co-founded, in 1985. Jobs took time away from the tech industry, reflecting on his journey and recalibrating his vision. During this period, he founded NeXT and acquired Pixar, both of which would go on to be massive successes in their own right. When Jobs returned to Apple in 1997, he was stronger and more focused than ever, leading the company through one of the most remarkable turnarounds in corporate history.

Similarly, Oprah Winfrey, one of the most influential media personalities in the world, has often spoken about the importance of rest and introspection in her success. After decades of intense work building her media empire, Oprah took a step back, dedicating time to personal reflection and spiritual growth. This period of rest allowed her to return with renewed purpose, leading to the creation of OWN: The Oprah Winfrey Network, a platform that aligns more closely with her personal mission of inspiring and empowering others.

These stories illustrate a common truth: Rest is not a retreat from greatness. It is the foundation upon which greater success is built.

The Science of Rest and Achievement

Scientific research supports the idea that rest enhances creativity, problem-solving, and long-term productivity. Studies show that the brain remains active during periods of rest, processing information and making connections that are not possible during periods of intense focus. This is why many people experience "aha" moments or breakthroughs when they are relaxed, whether during a walk, in the shower, or while daydreaming.

For example, Albert Einstein often credited his moments of relaxation and downtime for some of his most innovative ideas. His theory of relativity, one of the most significant scientific breakthroughs of the 20th century, emerged from a period of reflection and contemplation. Einstein understood that the mind needs time to wander and explore freely in order to make creative leaps.

Similarly, Thomas Edison, one of the most prolific inventors in history, was known for taking frequent naps throughout the day. He believed that these short periods of rest helped him stay sharp and maintain his creative edge. Edison's approach to rest allowed him to generate a remarkable number of inventions, including the lightbulb and the phonograph.

Embracing Strategic Rest for Greater Achievement

To rise strong after rest, it's essential to approach rest strategically. This means intentionally carving out time for rest and reflection, rather than waiting until burnout forces us to stop. Strategic rest involves planning regular breaks throughout our daily routines, as well as longer periods of rest, such as vacations or sabbaticals, to recharge and refocus.

Here are a few ways to embrace strategic rest in your life:

1. Prioritize Rest: Make rest a non-negotiable part of your schedule. Whether it's daily breaks, weekend getaways, or annual vacations, commit to giving yourself the time you need to recharge.

2. Reflect Regularly: Use periods of rest to reflect on your goals, values, and progress. This will help you stay aligned with your purpose and ensure that your efforts are focused on what truly matters.

3. Practice Mindfulness: Incorporate mindfulness practices, such as meditation or journaling, into your routine to enhance your self-awareness and clarity.

4. Embrace Breakthroughs: Trust that rest will lead to breakthroughs. Give yourself permission to step away from work, knowing that you will return stronger, more creative, and more focused.

Conclusion: Rest as the Foundation for Success

Strategic rest is not a luxury—it's a necessity for sustained success. By intentionally incorporating rest into our lives, we create the conditions for greater achievement, creativity, and purpose. The individuals who rise to the greatest heights are not those who work non-stop, but those who understand the power of rest and use it to their advantage.

Rest is not the end of the journey; it is the preparation for the next ascent. So, take a break, reflect, and rise stronger than ever before.

CHAPTER 14

SUSTAINING THE CYCLE
HOW TO INTEGRATE STRATEGIC REST INTO DAILY LIFE

We push ourselves to the limit, constantly chasing deadlines, dreams, and goals, while neglecting the very thing that could enhance our productivity and creativity: rest. But true success requires more than hard work—it requires balance. Integrating strategic rest into daily life is essential to maintaining long-term energy, focus, and creativity.

In this chapter, we will explore practical strategies to make rest a consistent part of your lifestyle, ensuring you can sustain high performance and well-being over time.

The Rest-Work Balance: A Key to Longevity

The key to achieving sustained success lies in balancing periods of intense work with periods of deliberate rest. Just as athletes alternate between training and recovery to avoid injury and optimize performance, we, too, must give our minds and bodies time to recover from daily stresses.

Burnout occurs when we ignore the signals our bodies send us, pushing through fatigue instead of replenishing our energy. Rest is not just about physical recovery but also about mental and emotional rejuvenation. The brain, like any other muscle, needs time to rest and reset. The question is not if we need rest, but how we can make rest a consistent part of our lives.

Practical Strategies for Daily Rest

1. Micro-Breaks During the Day: Incorporating short, strategic pauses throughout your workday can enhance focus and productivity. Research shows that the brain can maintain peak focus for about 90 minutes at a time, after which performance begins to decline. By scheduling regular micro-breaks—5 to 10 minutes every hour or two—you allow your mind to refresh, preventing fatigue and boosting creativity.

During these breaks, step away from your workspace. Take a short walk, stretch, practice deep breathing, or engage in a mindfulness exercise. These small moments of rest help maintain energy levels and improve cognitive function over the course of the day.

2. Create a Rest Ritual for the Evening: One of the best ways to wind down after a busy day is to establish a calming evening routine. This ritual signals to your body and mind that it's time to rest. It could include activities such as light reading, meditation, gentle yoga, or a warm bath.

To maximize the quality of your rest, avoid stimulating activities like scrolling through social media or watching intense TV shows right before bed. Prioritize activities that relax you and clear your mind, allowing you to ease into sleep more naturally.

3. Prioritize Sleep: Rest doesn't just mean taking breaks during the day—it also means prioritizing sleep. Despite the importance of sleep for mental clarity, emotional balance, and physical health, it's often one of the first things we sacrifice in the name of productivity.

To improve sleep quality, establish a consistent bedtime, create a sleep-friendly environment, and avoid caffeine and heavy meals close to bedtime. Aim for 7-9 hours of sleep each night to ensure that your body has the time it needs to repair and regenerate.

Weekly Rest Rituals for Recovery

While daily rest is essential, it's equally important to build in longer periods of recovery throughout the week. Many people find that dedicating one day each week to rest, reflection, and rejuvenation helps them recharge for the week ahead. This weekly rest ritual could take various forms depending on your personal preferences and responsibilities.

1. The Power of a Digital Detox: In an age where we are constantly connected to our devices, taking a break from technology can be deeply restorative. Dedicate one day each week—such as Sunday—to unplug from technology. Turn off your phone, step away from your computer, and spend time reconnecting with yourself, your loved ones, or nature. This digital detox gives your mind a break from the constant stream of information and helps you reset emotionally.

2. Engage in a Meaningful Hobby: Rest doesn't always mean doing nothing. Sometimes, the best way to recharge is by engaging in a hobby or activity that brings you joy. Whether it's painting, gardening, cooking, or hiking, spend one day each week doing something that fills you with a sense of fulfillment and relaxation. This allows you to tap into your creative side and restore your energy.

3. Reflect and Reset: Take time each week to reflect on your goals, your progress, and your overall well-being. Use this day to review the previous week and plan for the week ahead, making adjustments to your schedule to ensure you're balancing work and rest. Reflection helps you stay aligned with your purpose and allows you to approach the new week with clarity and intention.

The Power of Yearly Sabbaticals

In addition to daily and weekly rest, consider the long-term benefits of taking an extended break—a sabbatical—from your regular responsibilities. A sabbatical can be anything from a few weeks to several months, depending on your personal or professional circumstances. The purpose of a sabbatical is to step away from your day-to-day tasks and immerse yourself in activities that refresh your mind, body, and spirit.

1. Reconnecting with Nature: Many people use their sabbaticals to reconnect with nature, whether through travel or extended outdoor retreats. Time spent in natural settings has been shown to reduce stress, improve mood, and increase creativity. Consider taking a hiking trip, visiting a remote location, or simply spending more time outdoors during your sabbatical to gain a fresh perspective on your life and work.

2. Focus on Personal Growth: Sabbaticals are also an opportunity for personal growth. You can use this time to pursue a new skill, learn a language, or explore a creative project you've always wanted to undertake. By focusing on personal development during your sabbatical, you'll return to your regular life with a renewed sense of purpose and achievement.

3. Reflect on Your Long-Term Goals: Sabbaticals provide a unique opportunity to reflect on your long-term goals. Often, we get so caught up in the day-to-day grind that we lose sight of the bigger picture. Use your sabbatical to think deeply about your personal and professional aspirations. What do you truly want to achieve? Are you on the right path? This time away from your routine can provide the clarity needed to realign your life with your goals.

Periodic Unplugging: Essential for Mental and Emotional Health

The constant bombardment of information from digital devices can lead to mental fatigue and overwhelm. Periodic unplugging from technology is not only beneficial but essential for maintaining emotional balance and mental clarity.

1. Schedule Regular "No-Tech" Days: In addition to weekly digital detoxes, consider scheduling longer "no-tech" periods throughout the year. These could be weekend getaways or even week-long vacations where you intentionally leave your devices behind. The absence of technology allows you to be more present, enjoy the moment, and engage in meaningful conversations and experiences without distractions.

2. Set Boundaries with Technology: You don't need to wait for vacations to unplug. Setting daily boundaries with technology—such as turning off notifications during meals or setting a time limit for social media—helps create space for rest and reflection. By controlling your digital habits, you prevent technology from taking over your life and mental energy.

Conclusion: A Lifestyle of Strategic Rest

The key to sustaining long-term energy, creativity, and productivity is to make rest a consistent part of your life, rather than something you resort to only in times of exhaustion. By incorporating daily micro-breaks, weekly rituals, and longer sabbaticals, you create a cycle of work and rest that allows you to thrive.

Rest is not a reward for hard work—it is a necessary part of the process. When you prioritize strategic rest, you not only maintain your energy but also enhance your creativity, focus, and resilience. By embracing rest as a critical part of your lifestyle, you empower yourself to achieve greater success and fulfillment over the long term.

In the end, integrating rest into your life is not about slowing down; it's about ensuring you have the strength and clarity to rise higher.

CHAPTER 15

CONCLUSION
RISE TO YOUR FULLEST POTENTIAL

As we come to the end of this journey through the art of strategic hibernation, it is essential to reflect on the wisdom that has emerged. We began by challenging the dominant culture of constant hustle and the belief that success comes only through unrelenting effort. Throughout this book, we have explored the transformative power of rest—not as a retreat from ambition but as a vital tool for preparing ourselves to achieve our fullest potential.

The path to success, both personally and professionally, is not a straight line. It involves cycles of work and rest, action and reflection, hustle and hibernation. Rest is not a sign of weakness or laziness; it is a strategic decision that allows you to recharge, regain perspective, and return with greater energy and clarity. The most successful people, from athletes to artists to entrepreneurs, have all recognized this truth.

The Journey of Strategic Hibernation

From the first chapter, we set out to redefine rest as a necessary and empowering part of life. We discovered how intentional pauses, like periods of hibernation, allow us to recalibrate and approach our work with renewed vigor. Along the way, we explored how rest enhances creativity, drives innovation, and even helps us push back against burnout in a world that values productivity above all else.

Through real-world examples, historical figures, and practical strategies, we've learned that rest is not about escaping responsibility or ambition—it's about giving yourself the space to grow, to reflect, and to rise stronger. Whether it's a quick micro-break during a busy day, a weekly ritual of rest and reflection, or a longer sabbatical, the strategic pauses we take are moments of empowerment, not retreat.

The Power of Rest to Achieve Your Potential

At its core, the message of this book is simple: rest is not the opposite of productivity—it's the key to unlocking your greatest potential. Just as nature uses periods of dormancy to grow stronger, so too must we incorporate rest into our lives if we are to rise to new heights.

In every chapter, we have seen the incredible outcomes that come from strategic rest. From the breakthroughs that emerge during moments of stillness to the personal growth found in the art of doing nothing, rest is an essential part of rising to our fullest potential. The greatest achievements, innovations, and creative solutions often come after intentional pauses. It is in these moments of quiet that clarity, vision, and purpose are restored.

Trusting the Process of Strategic Pauses

To truly rise, we must trust in the process of resting. It requires a shift in mindset—a rejection of the hustle culture that tells us we must always be "on" and productive. Instead, we must embrace the truth that rest is not an indulgence; it is a preparation. By strategically incorporating rest into our lives, we can achieve a balance that allows for both high performance and sustained well-being.

A Call to Action: Plan for Rest

As you close this book, the final call to action is simple but profound: make rest a priority in your life. Actively schedule rest periods—whether they are short breaks during your workday, full days of unplugging and reflection, or longer sabbaticals. Don't wait until you are exhausted or burned out to take a break. Instead, be proactive and plan for rest as a necessary component of your growth.

1. **Schedule It:** Put rest on your calendar, just as you would any important meeting or task. By doing so, you acknowledge its importance and give yourself permission to pause.

2. **Trust the Process:** Know that rest is not wasted time. It is part of the cycle that prepares you for the next phase of your journey. Trust that the time you spend resting will return to you tenfold in the form of renewed energy, creativity, and focus.

3. **Share the Message:** As you embrace the art of strategic hibernation, encourage others around you to do the same. By advocating for rest as a tool for success, you help shift the culture away from burnout and toward balance.

Rise to Your Fullest Potential

In the end, rest is about more than simply recharging—it's about preparing for the next phase of your life. When you prioritize rest, you equip yourself to rise stronger, think clearer, and achieve more. It is in the moments of stillness that you gather the strength needed to pursue your dreams with renewed passion.

As you move forward, remember that the journey to success is not a sprint—it's a marathon. And like any marathon, it requires pacing, moments of pause, and periods of recovery. Embrace rest as an essential part of that journey, and rise to your fullest potential with the power of strategic hibernation.

Now, it's your turn: pause, rest, and rise.

www.ingramcontent.com/pod-product-compliance
Lightning Source LLC
LaVergne TN
LVHW021159160826
845679LV00024B/2167

* 9 7 9 8 8 9 5 8 8 7 7 8 3 *